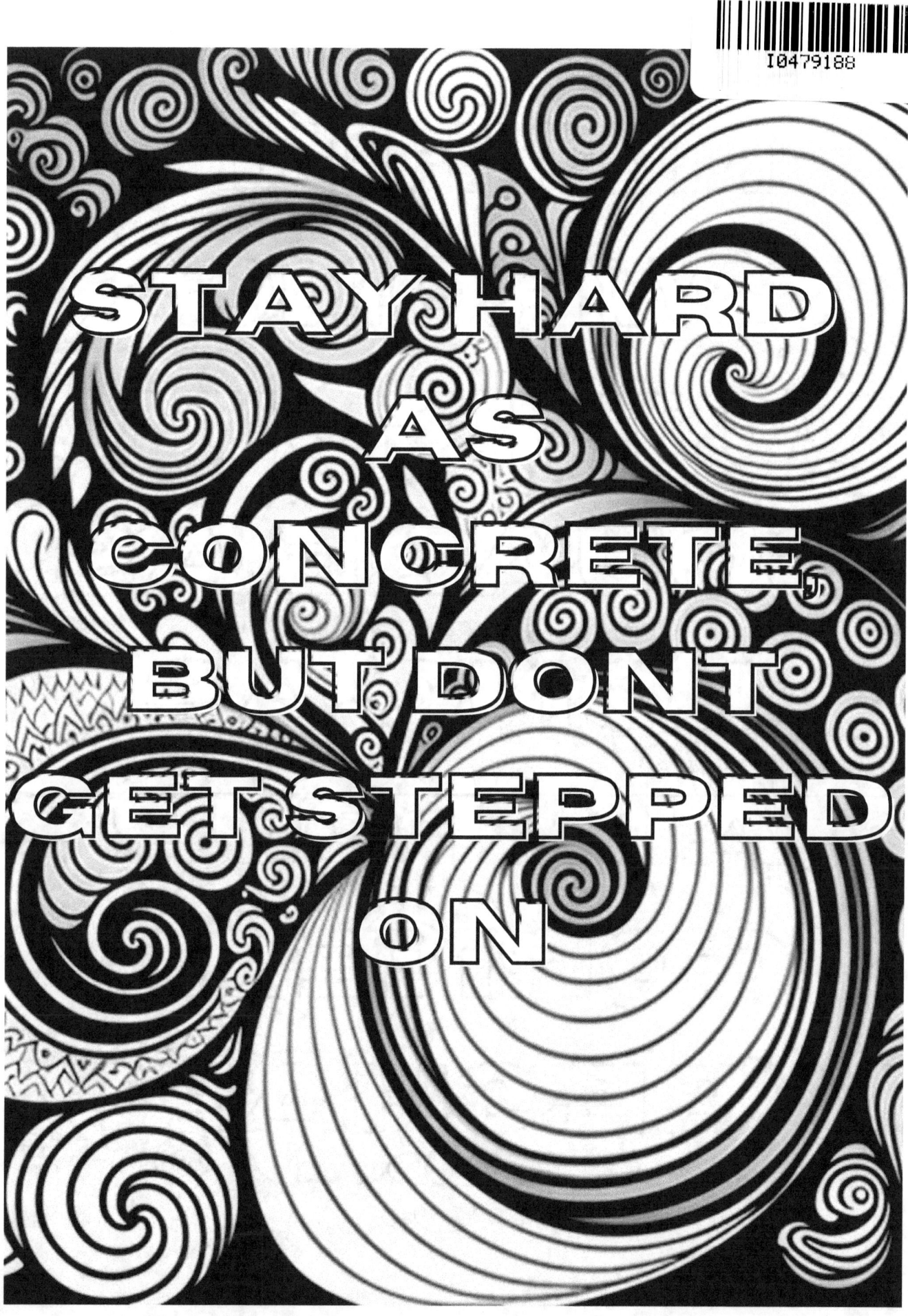

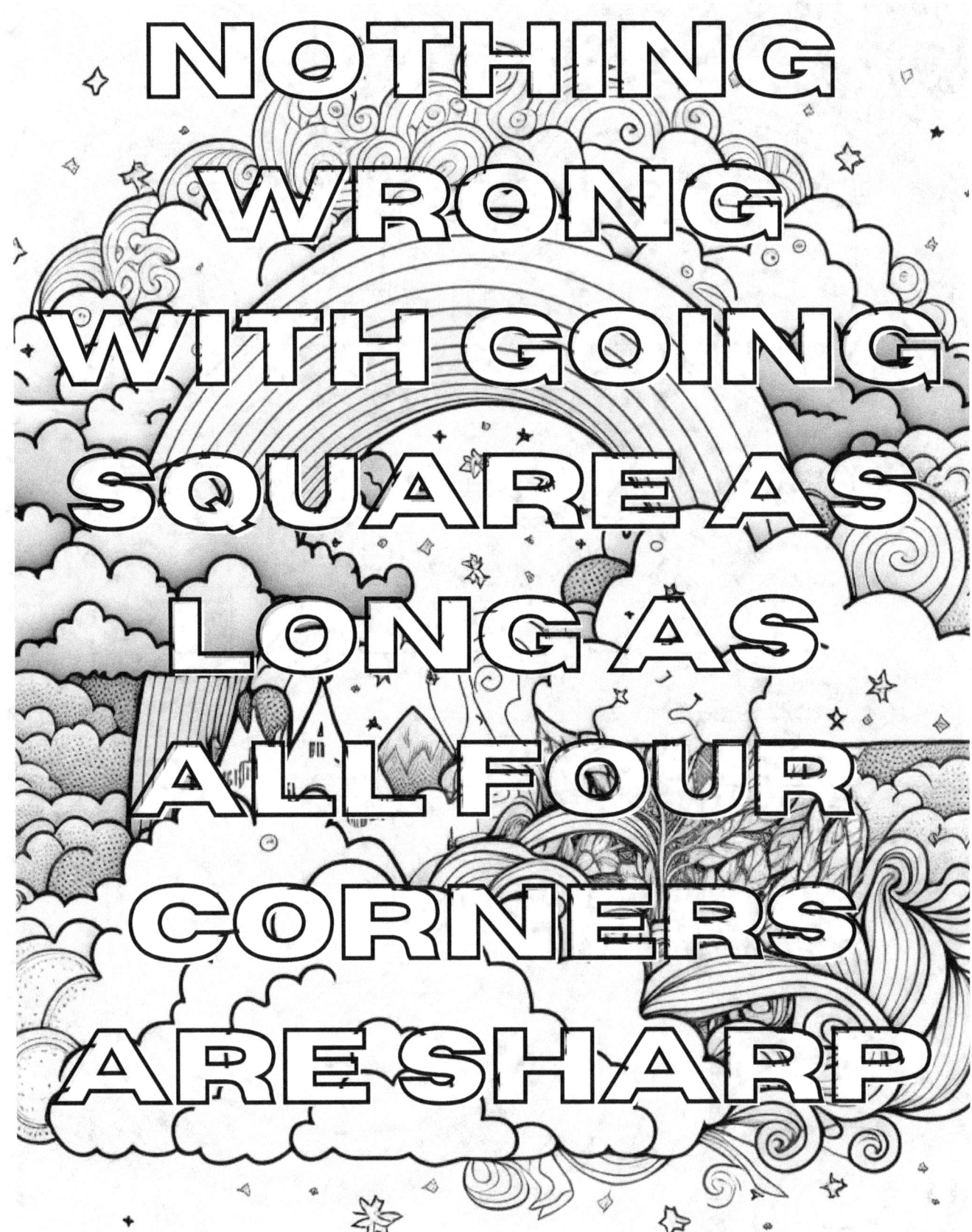

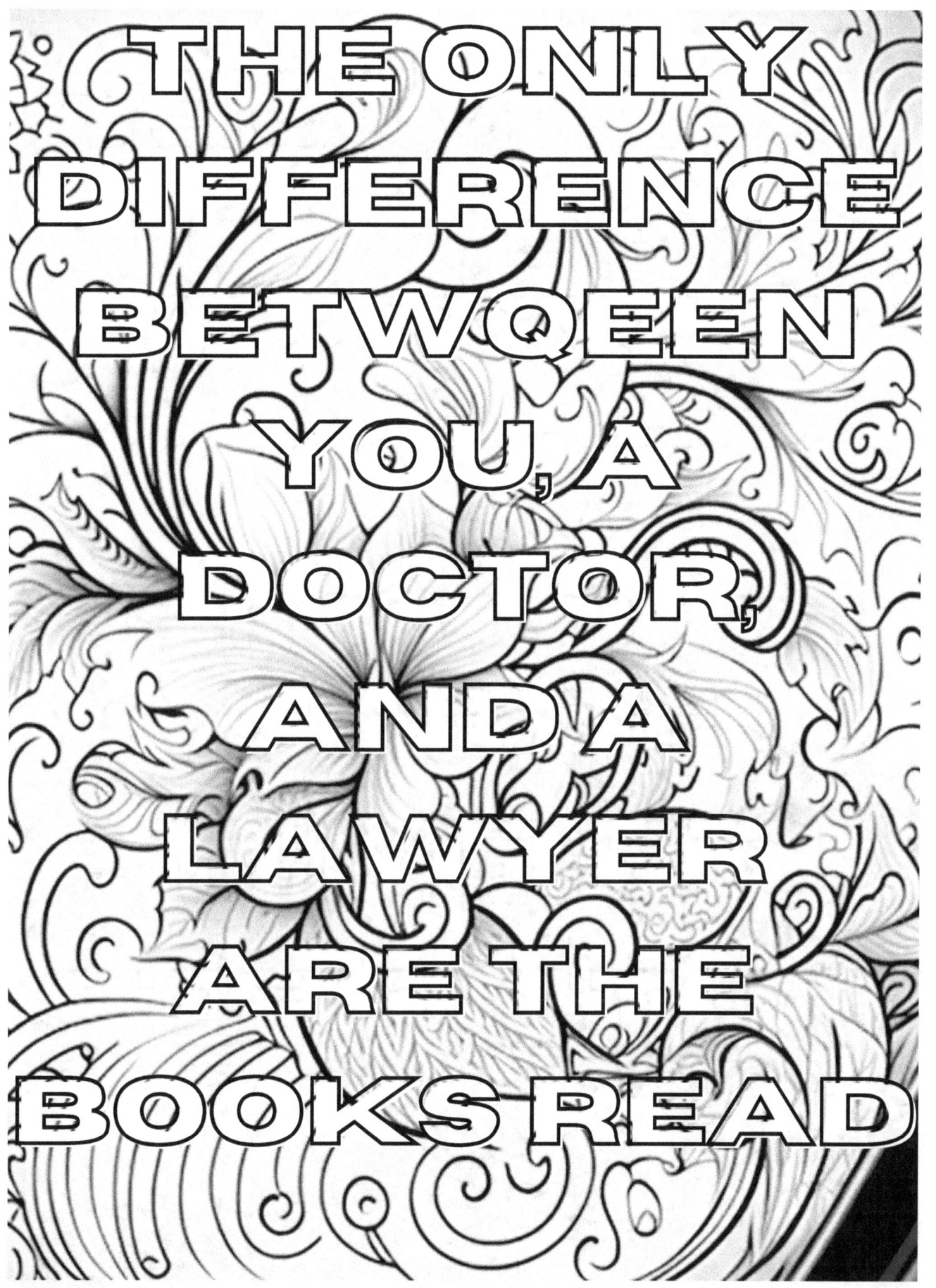

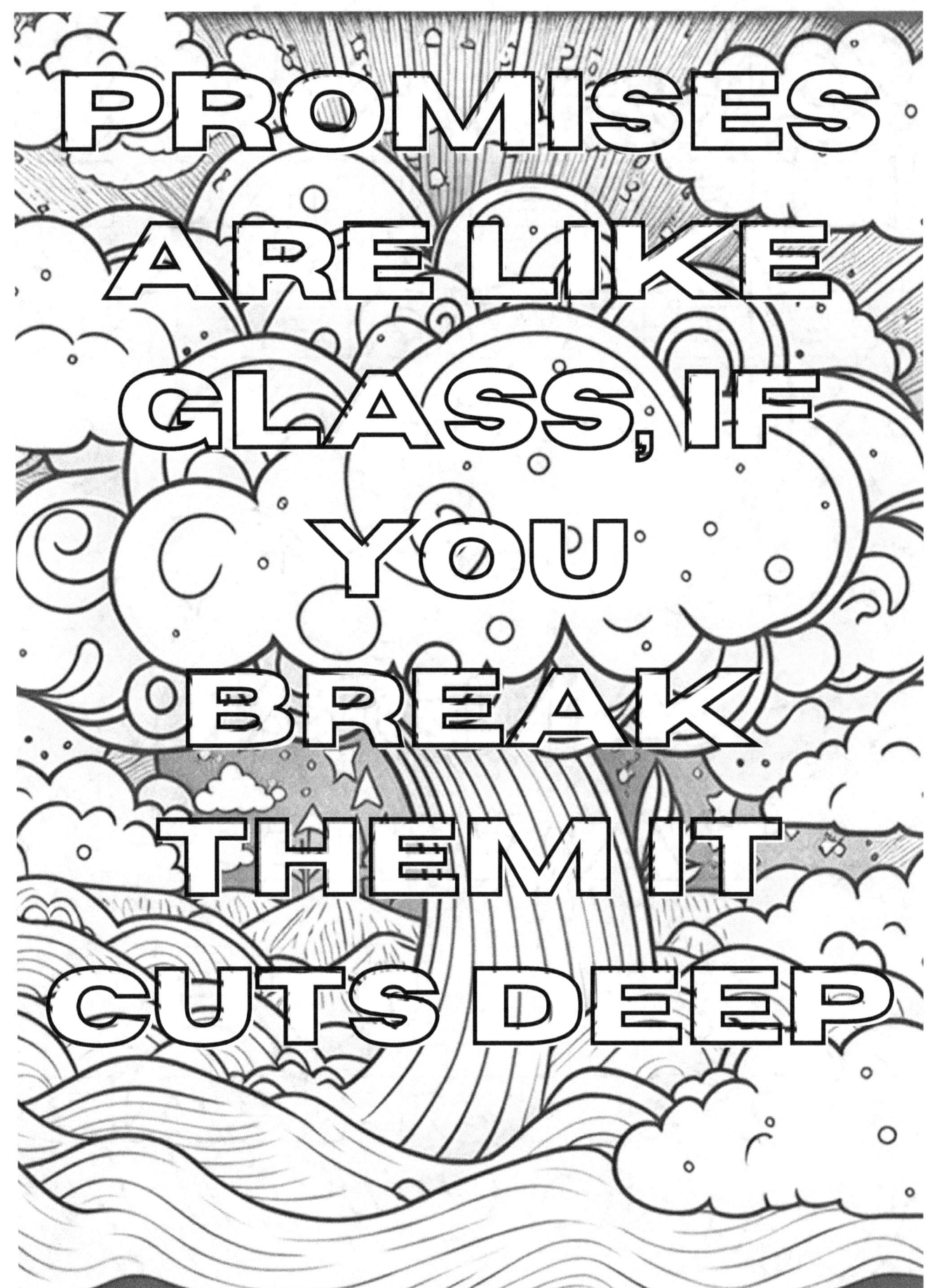

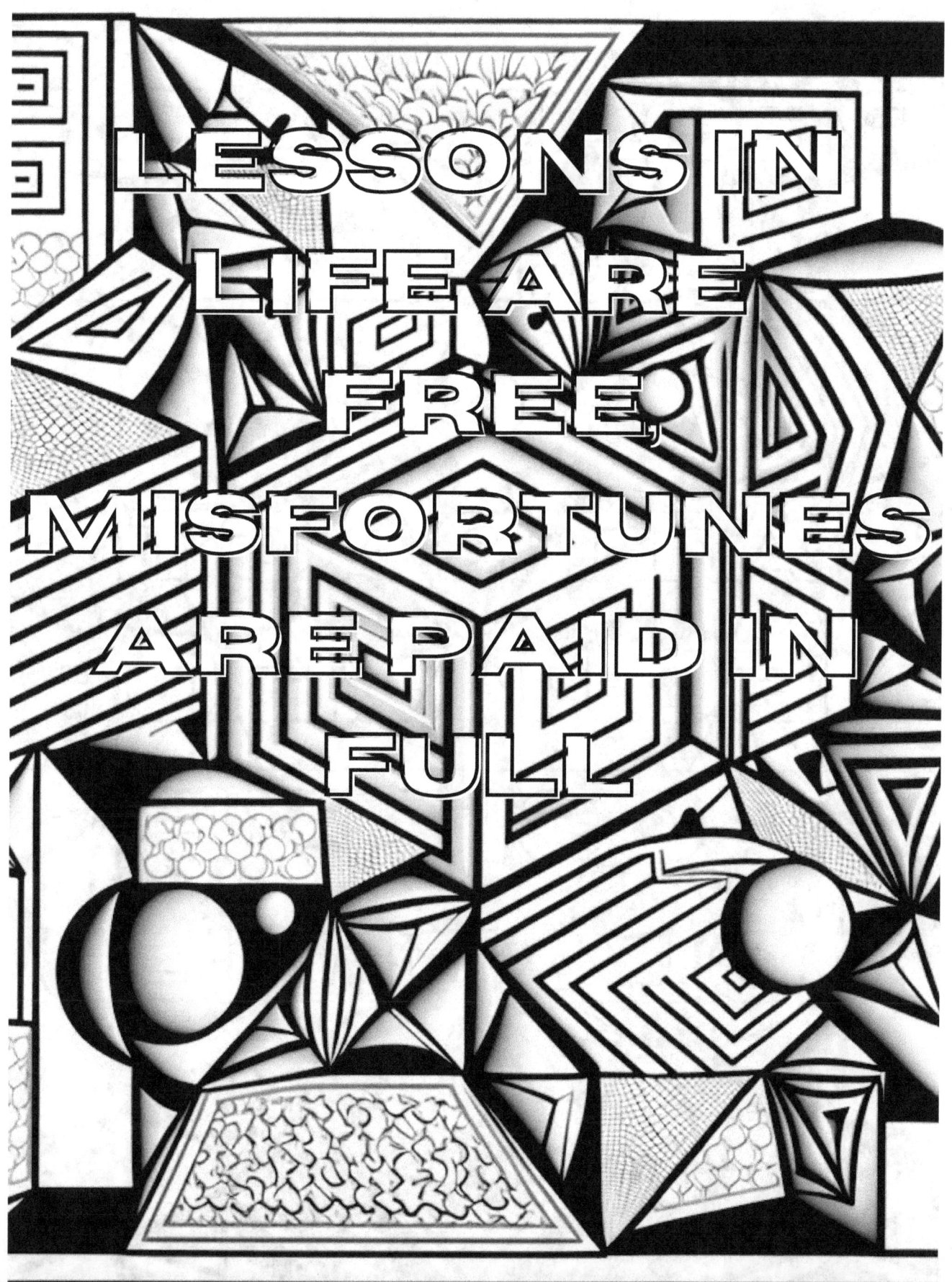

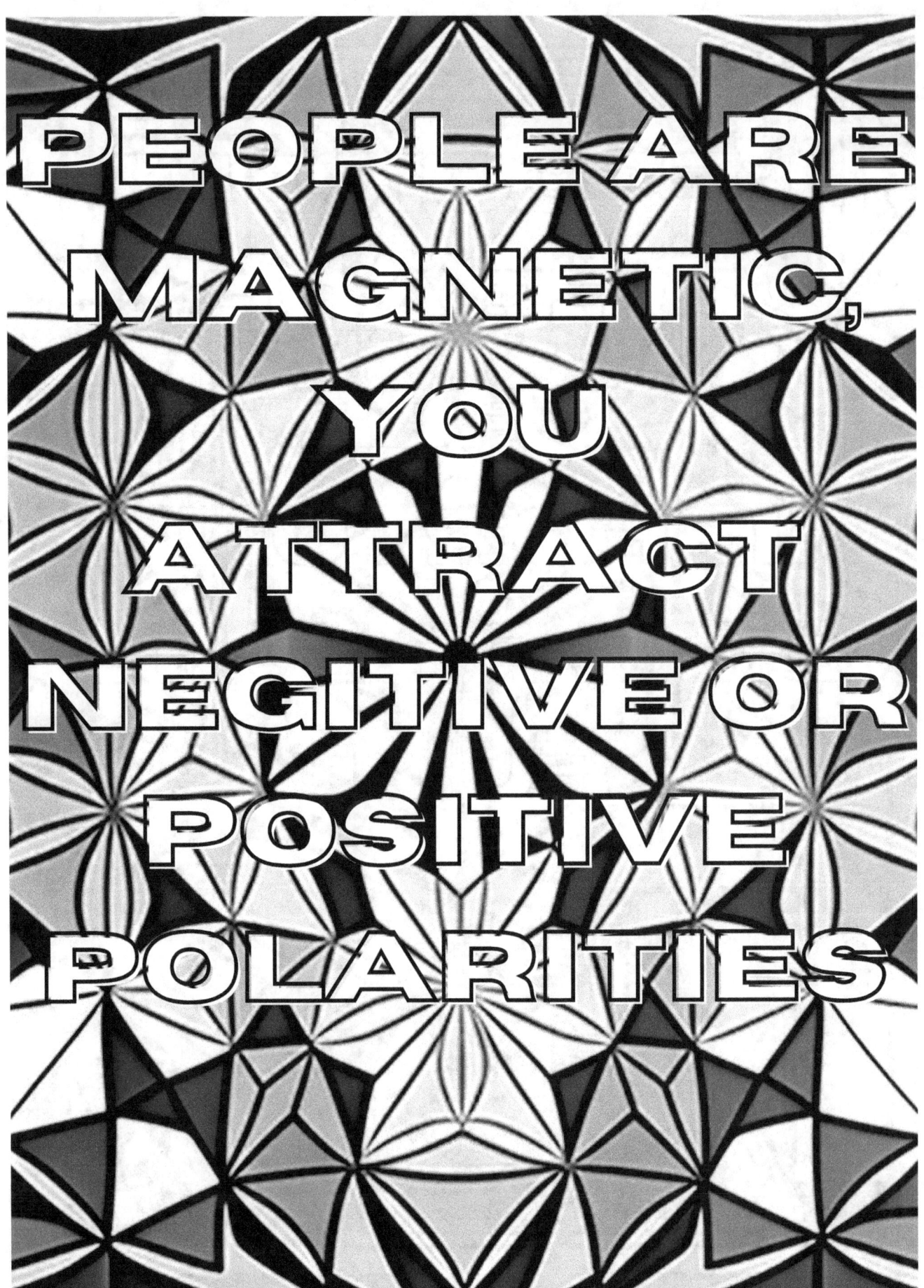

PEOPLE ARE MAGNETIC, YOU ATTRACT NEGITIVE OR POSITIVE POLARITIES

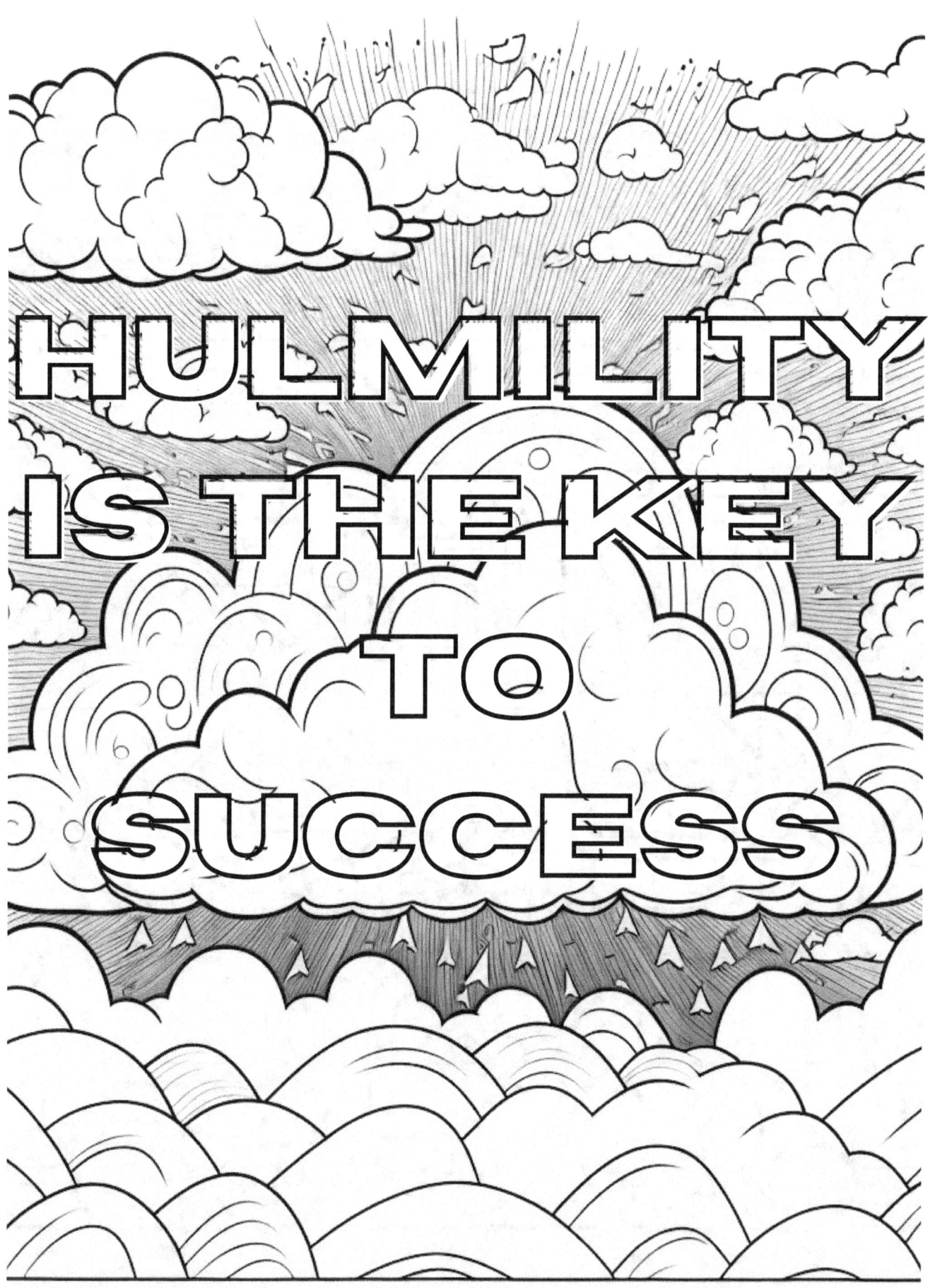

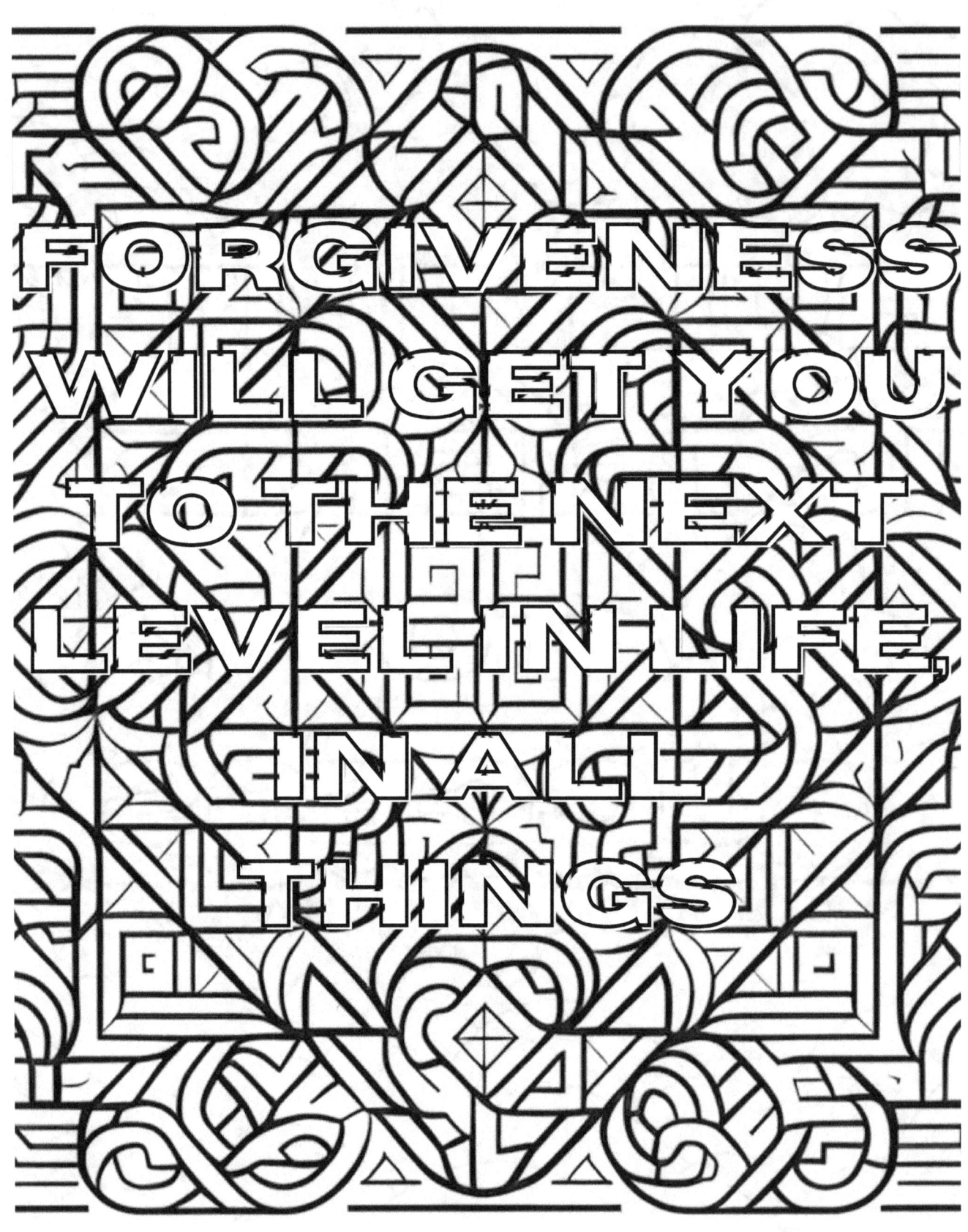

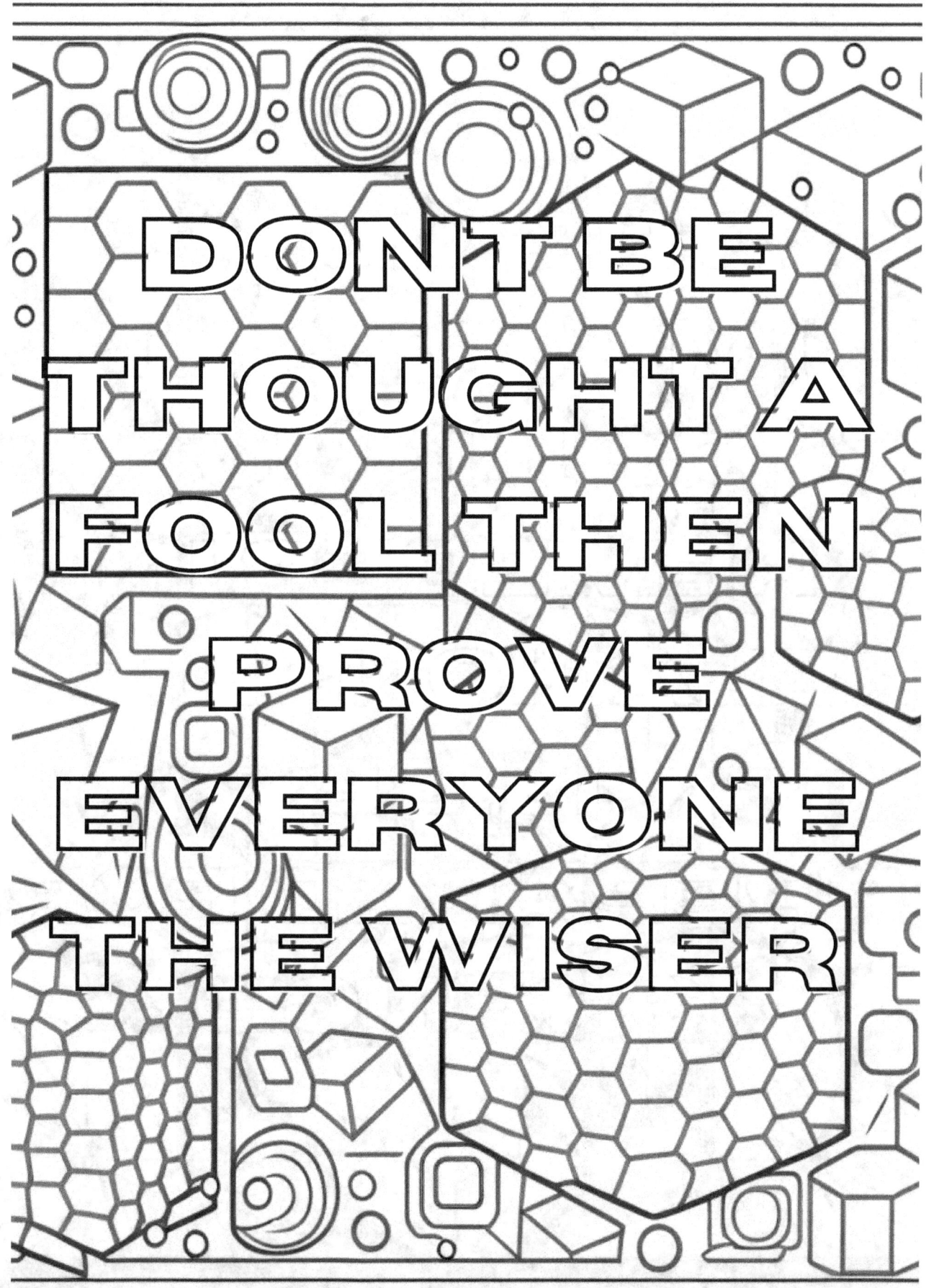

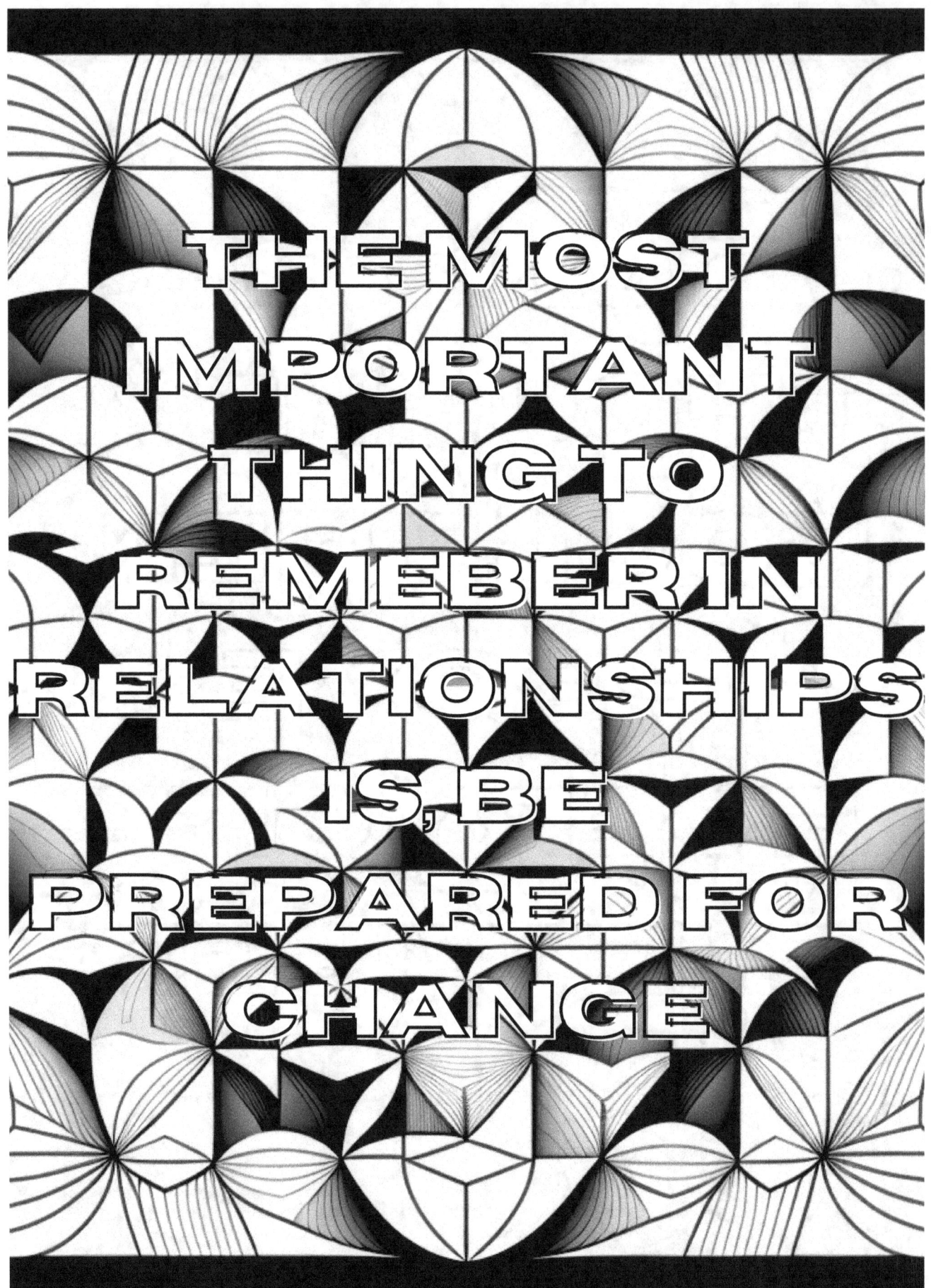

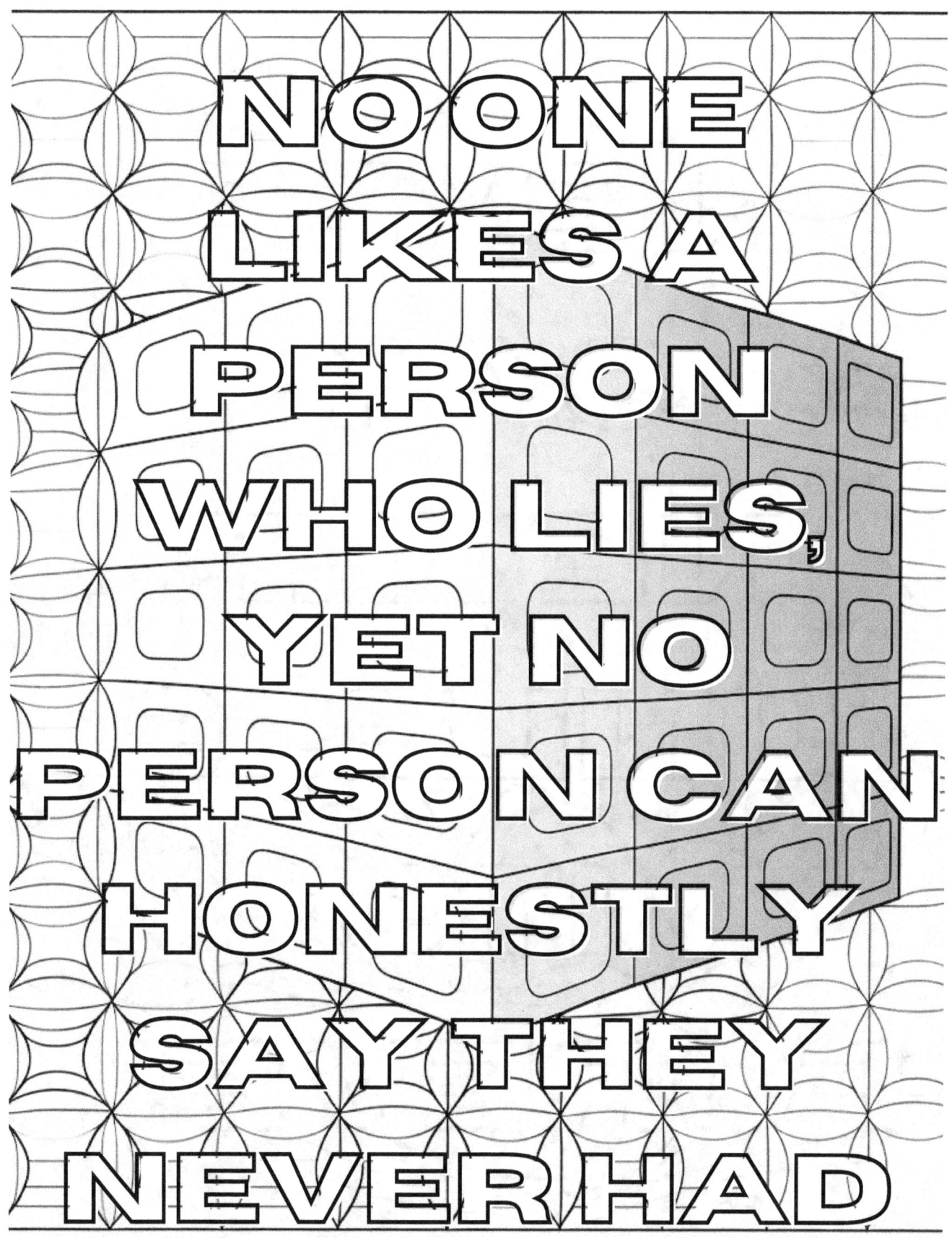

NO ONE LIKES A PERSON WHO LIES, YET NO PERSON CAN HONESTLY SAY THEY NEVER HAD

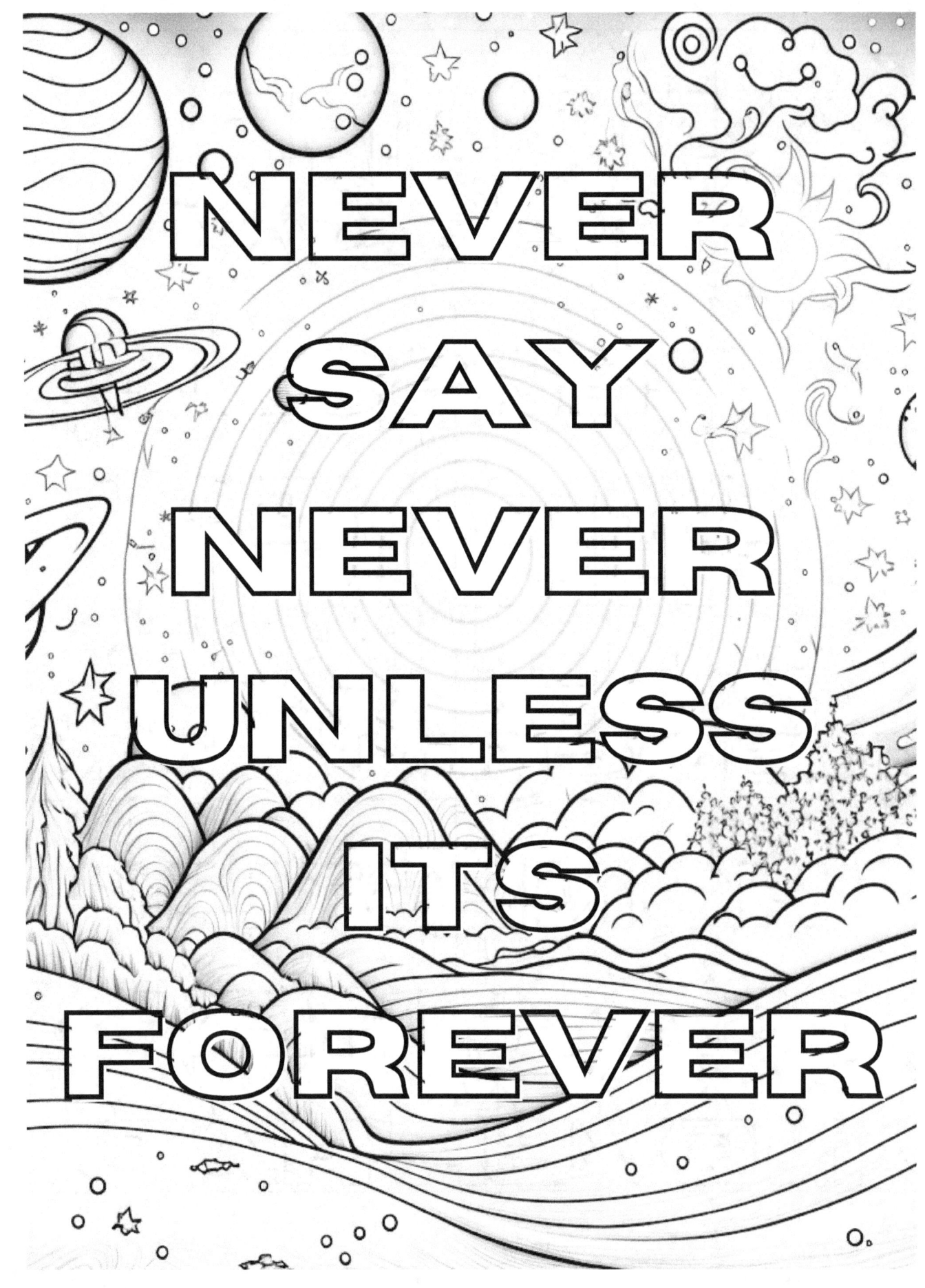

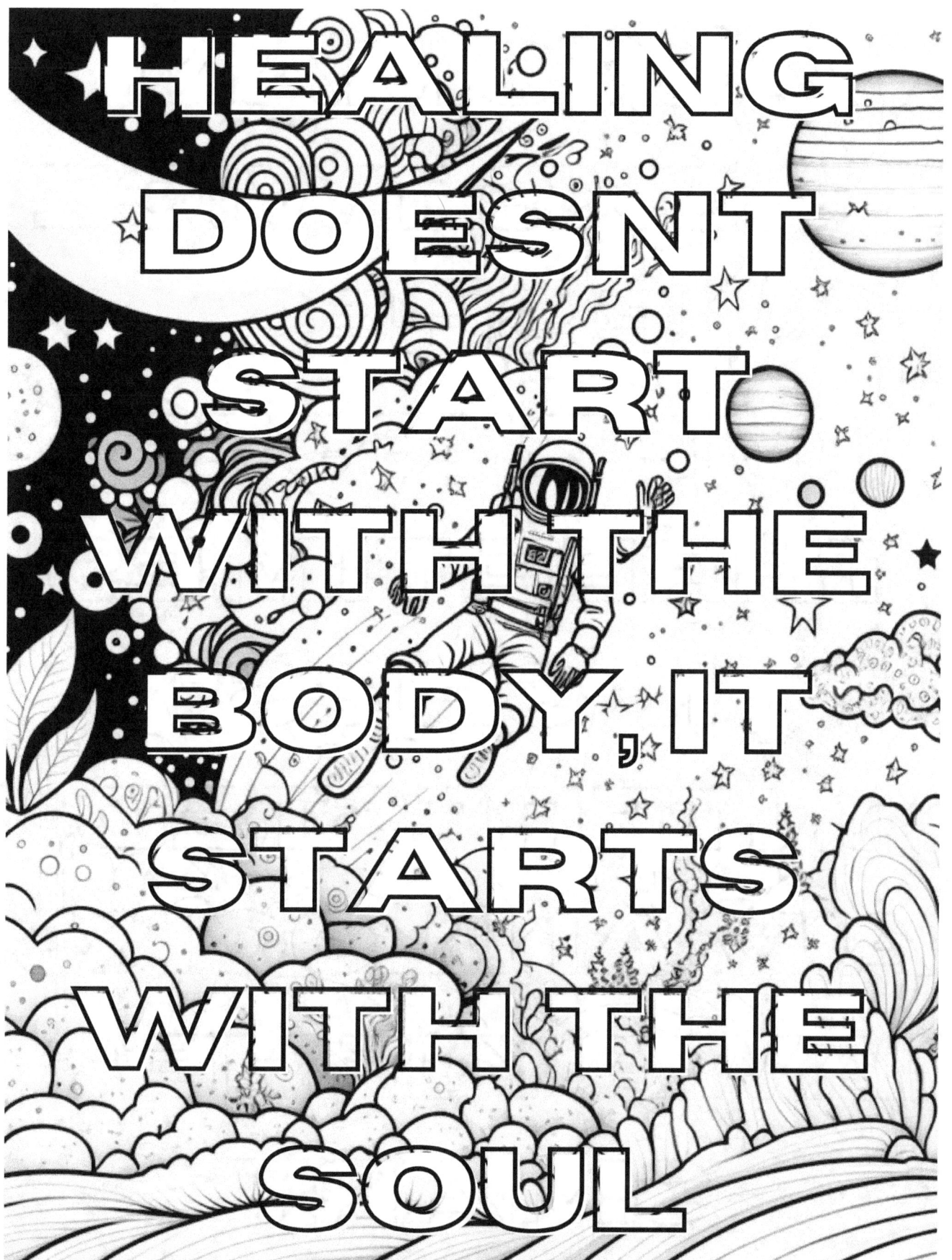

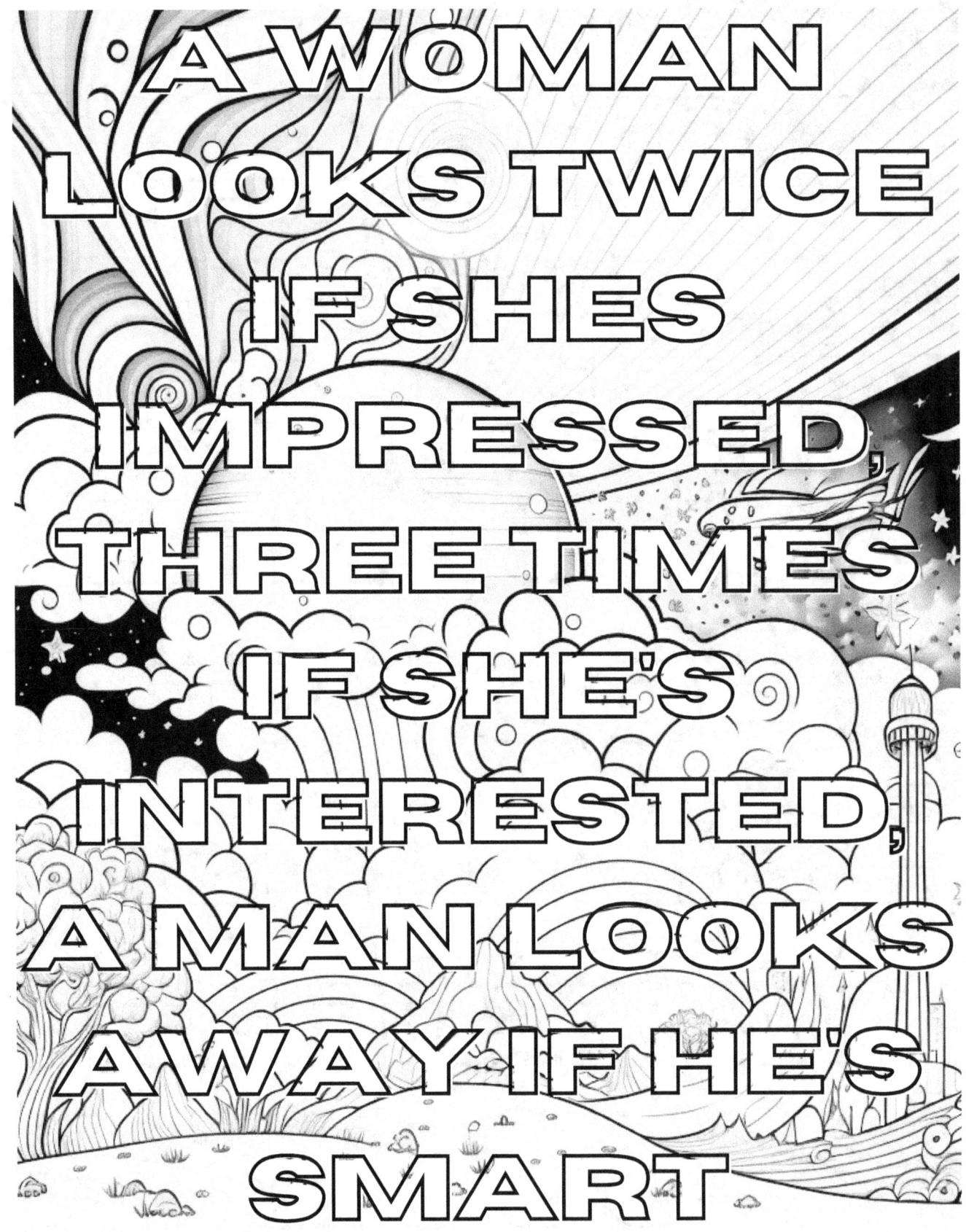

THE BRIGHTER THE LIGHT, THE CLOSER TO HOME

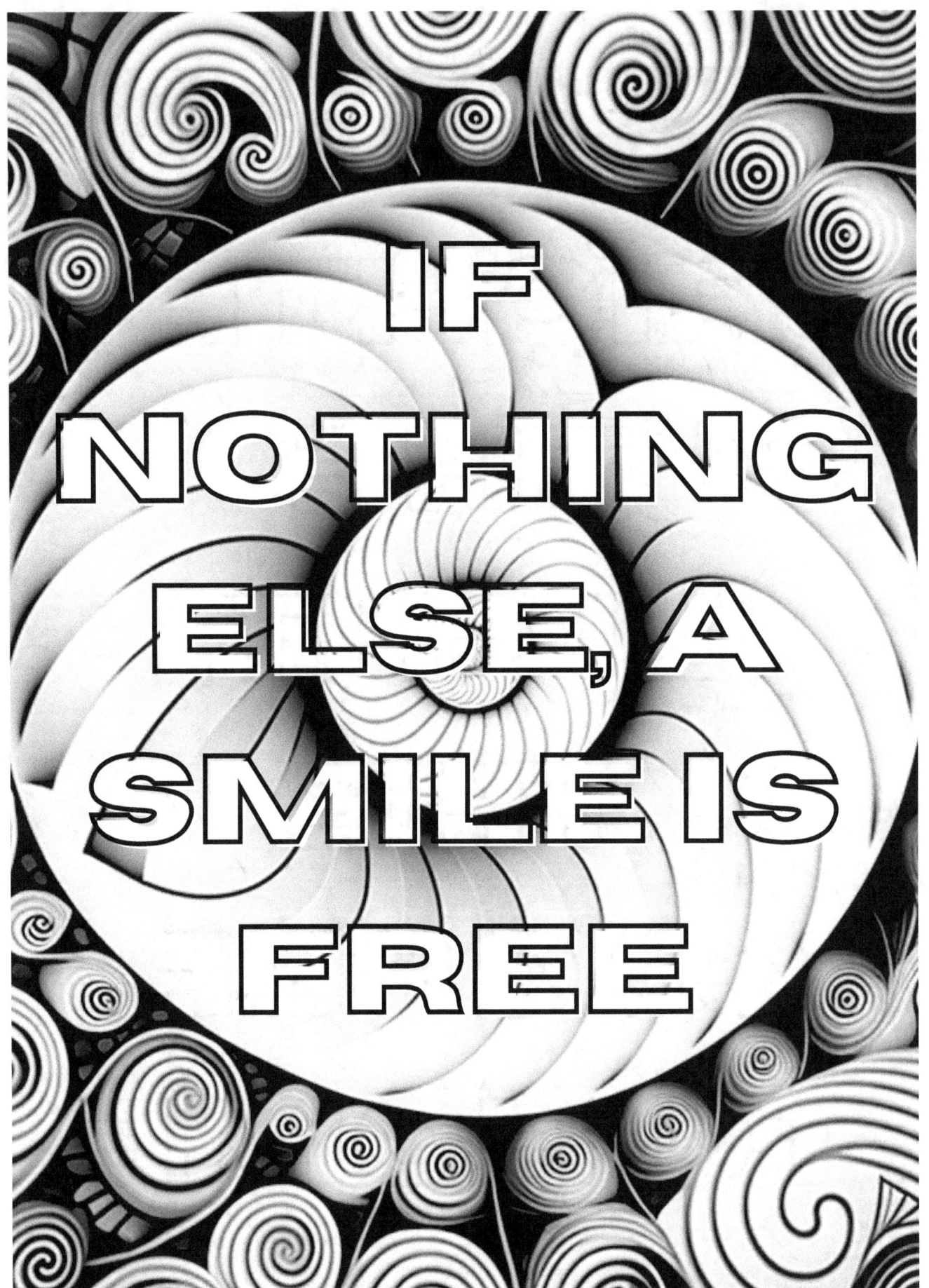

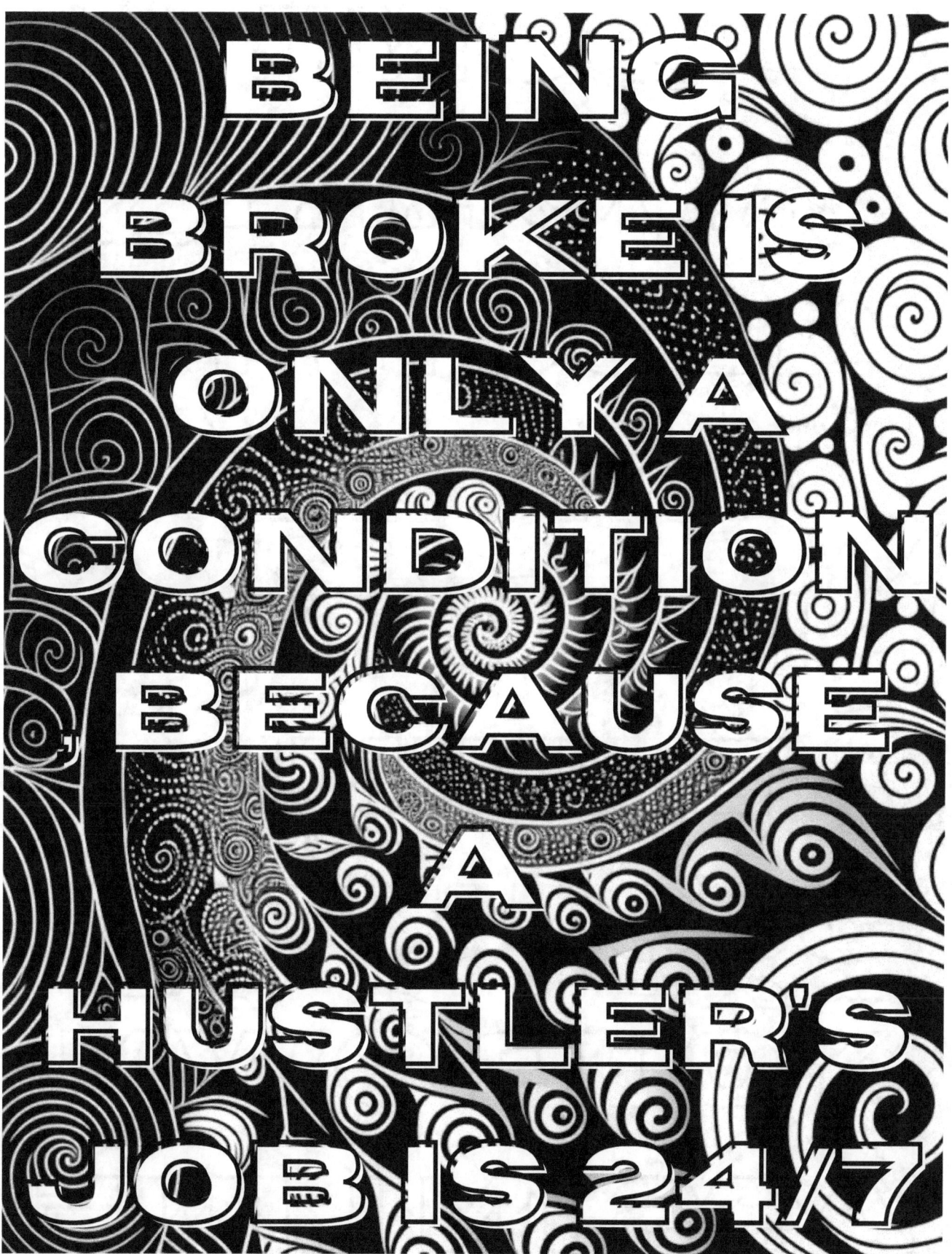

BEING BROKE IS ONLY A CONDITION BECAUSE A HUSTLER'S JOB IS 24/7

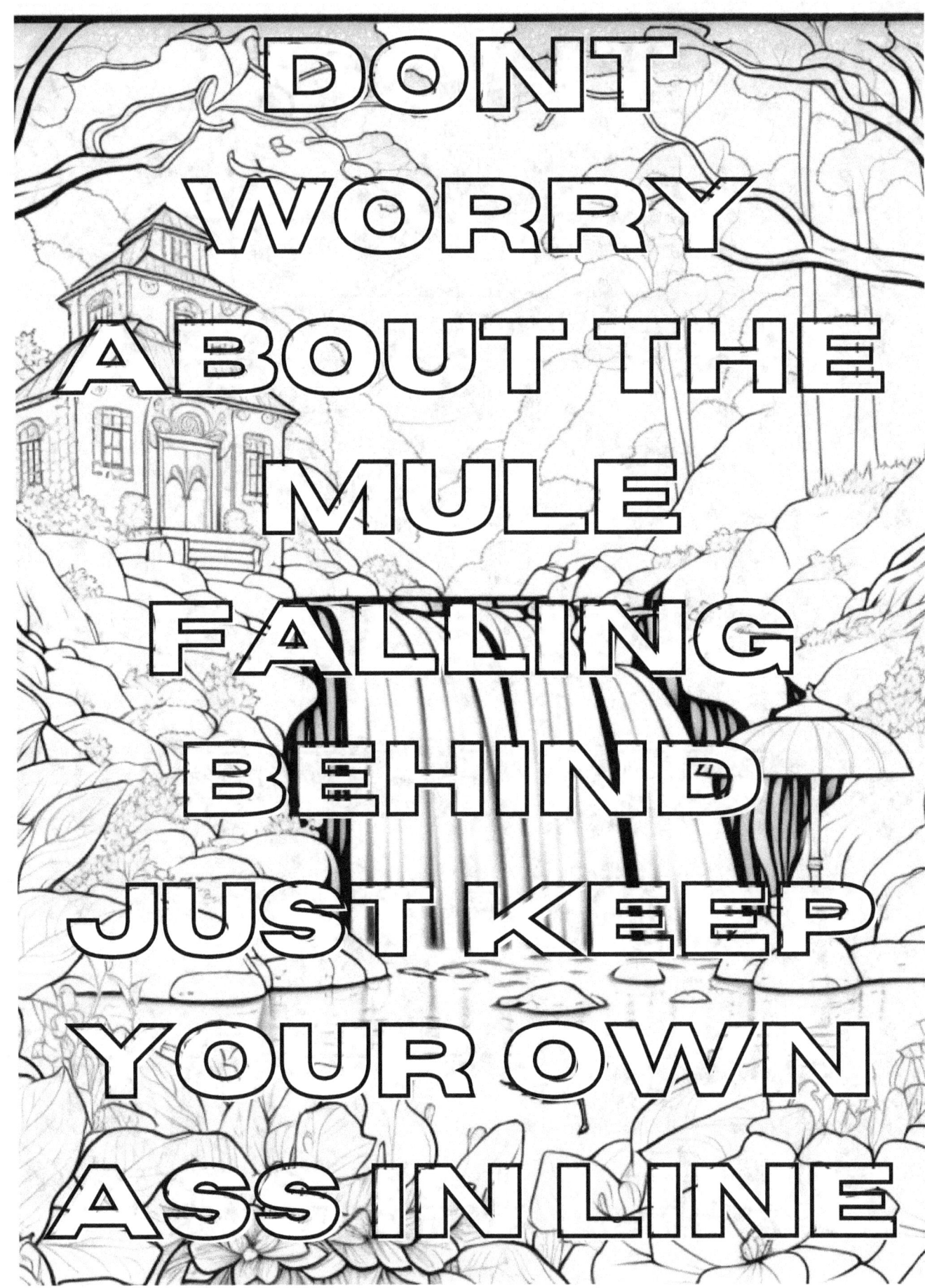

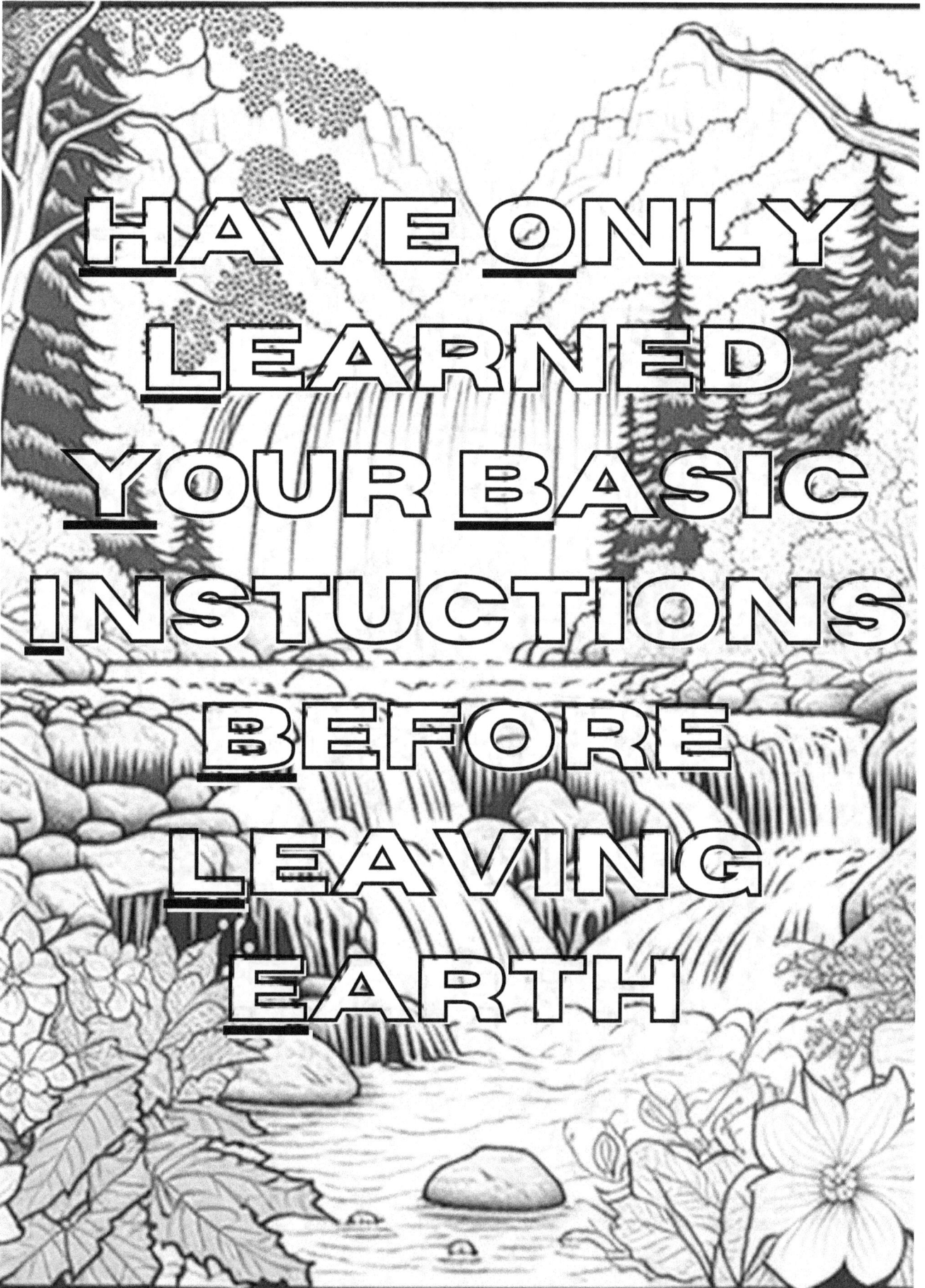

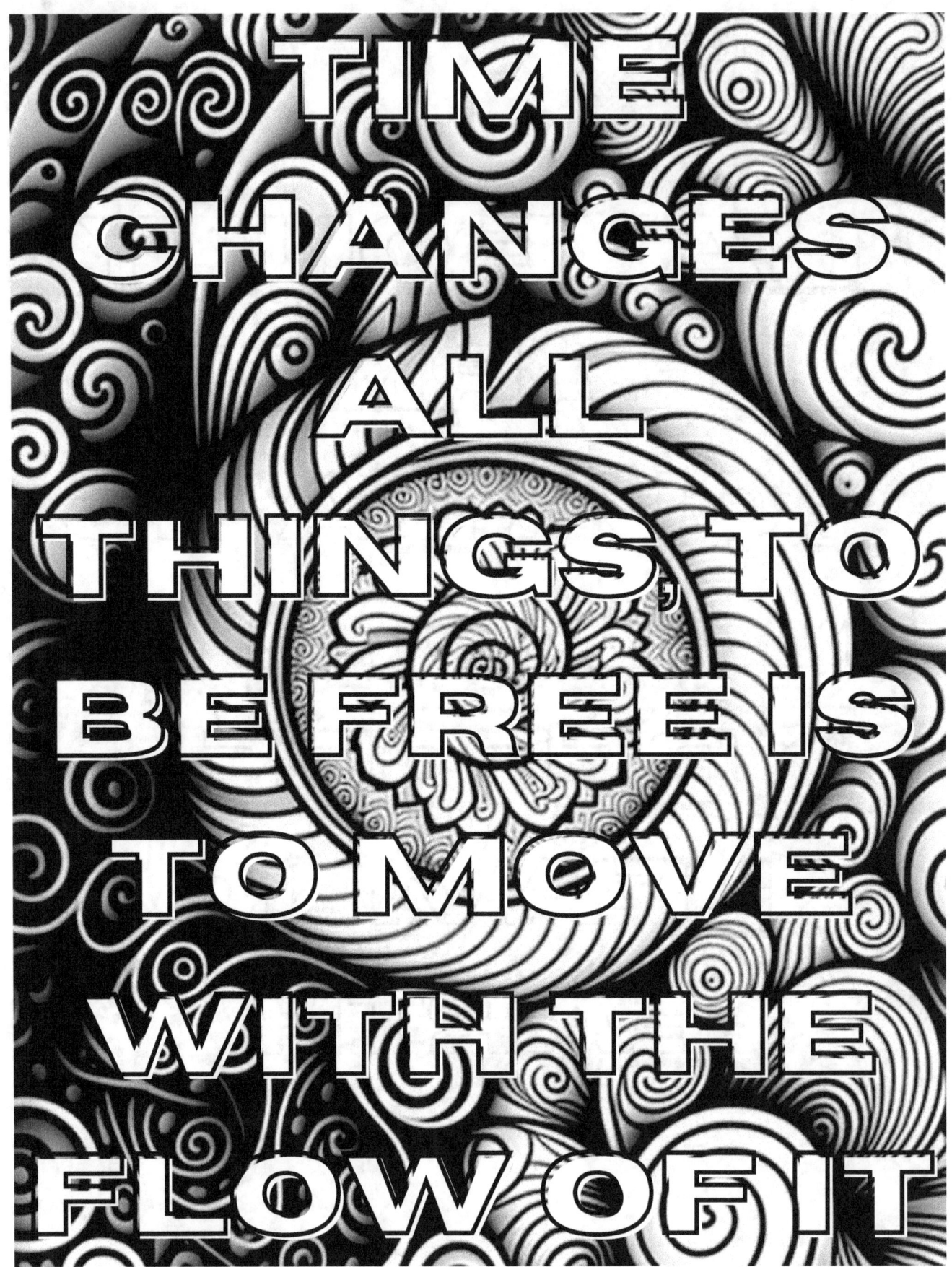

LIFE IS WHAT YOU HAVE, DEATH IS WHAT YOU GET, THE JOURNEY IS WHAT YOU CHOOSE

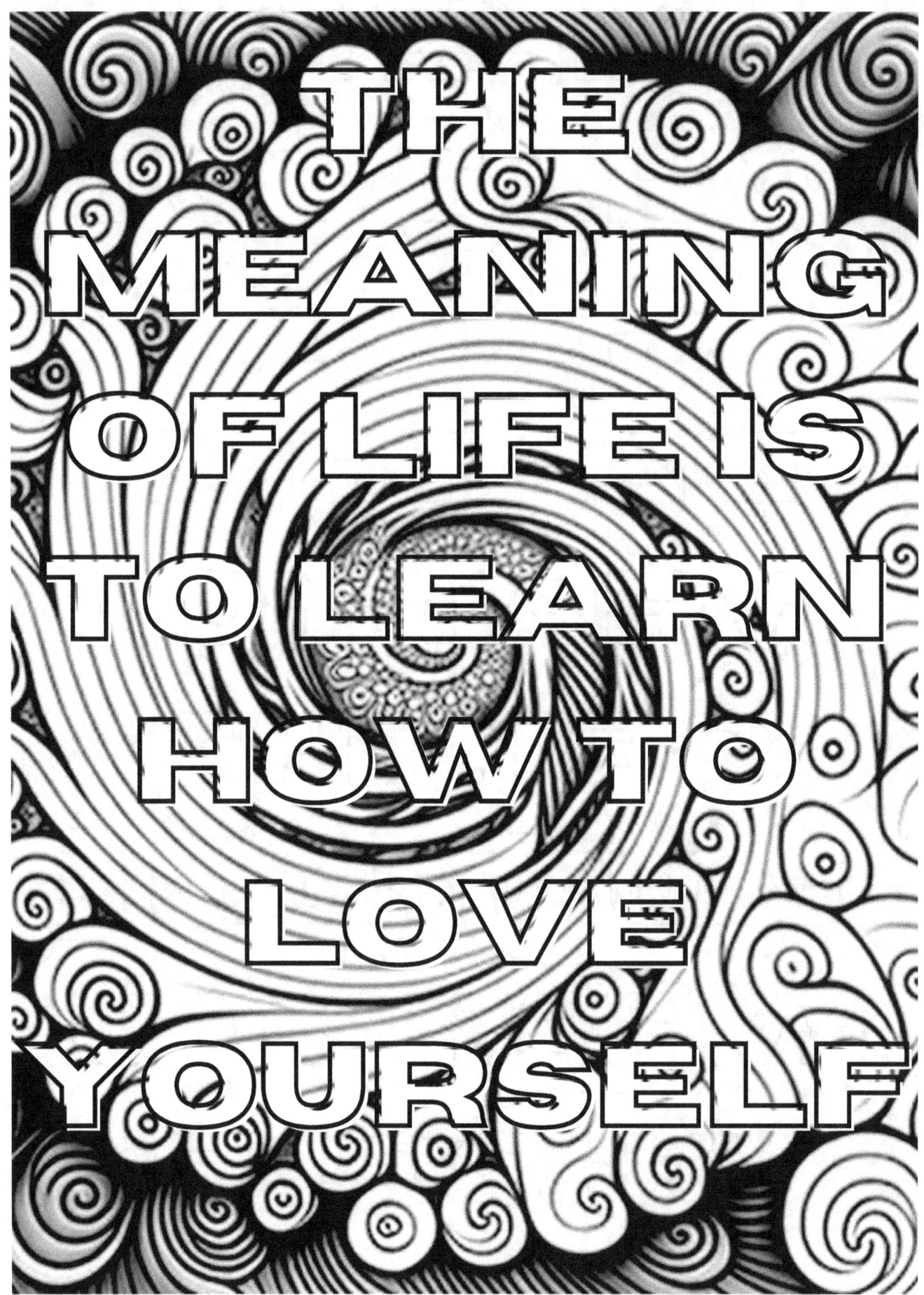

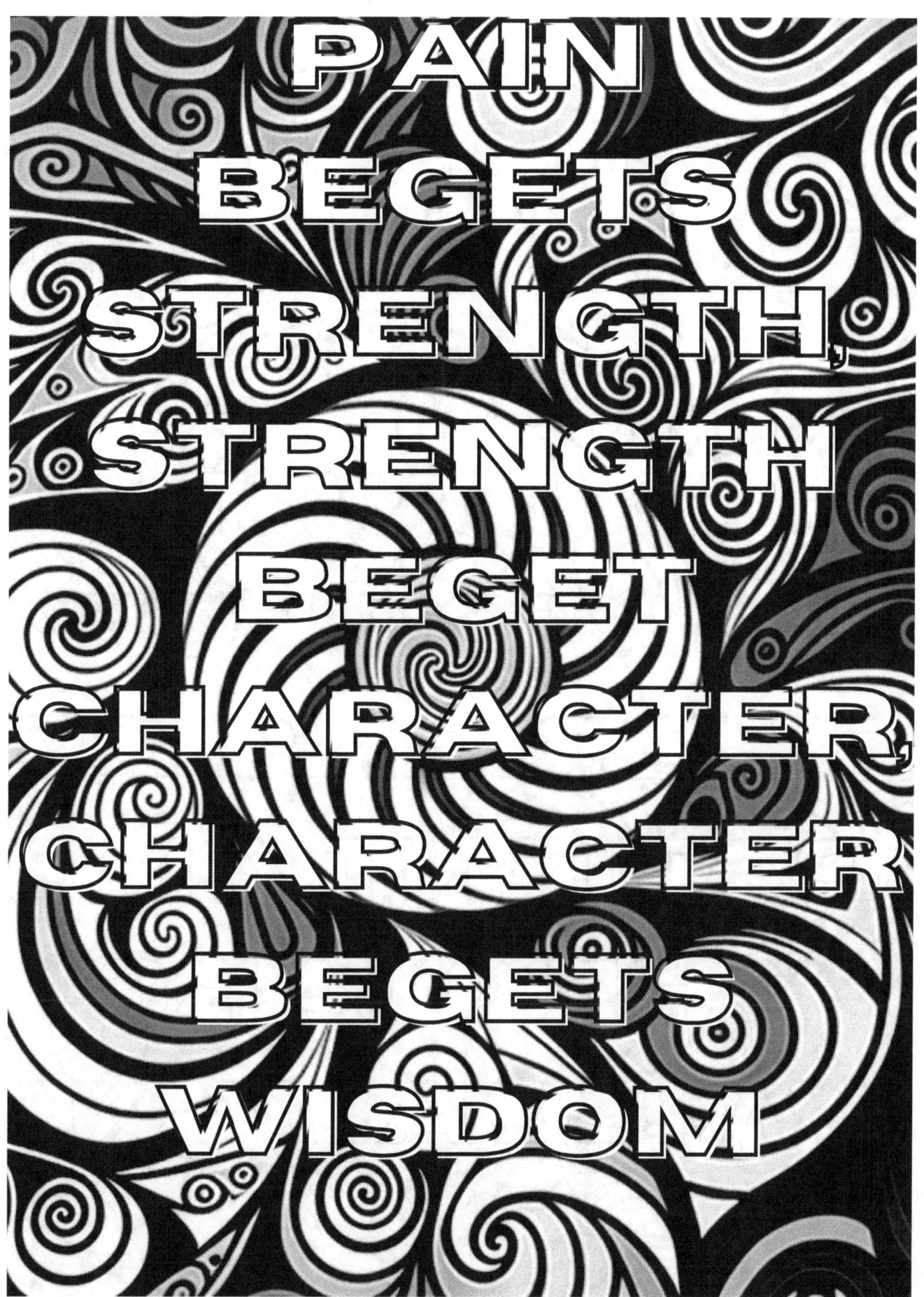

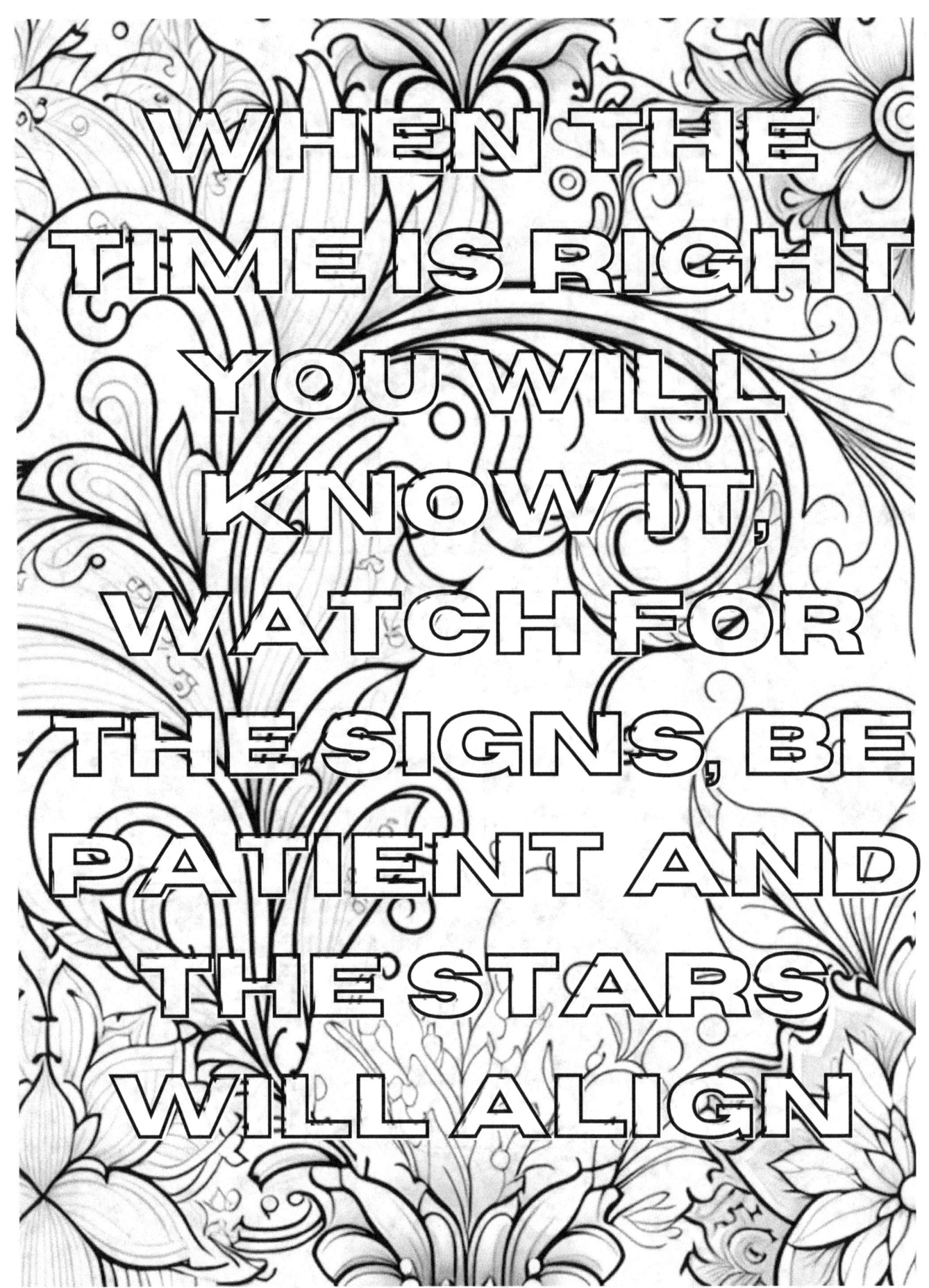